ISBN: 9798406229668

First Edition February 2022

Written for all the kids who feel forgotten, you are loved and your story matters.
Special thanks to my sweet husband,
Joe Ignace, for loving me and endlessly supporting me.
Thank you to my mom, Kelly Keehner,
who has the biggest heart and has been my biggest cheerleader.
Thank you to my mentor and life long friend, Shea Payne,
who showed me what it looks like to be a loving foster parent.
Thank you to the Norton family for sponsoring my book
and having a heart for foster care.

This book belongs to:

- -

self-portrait

My favorite person:

- -

self-portrait

Lily lived in a home with lots of fighting.
Her mommy and daddy hurt each other and yelled mean things.
Lily sometimes got scared and hid under her covers.

Lily's best friend was her dog Coco. Coco protected
Lily and barked when her mommy and daddy got angry.
Lily liked playing with Coco outside away from the yelling.

One day the yelling got really loud, so Lily went outside with Coco.
Lily heard lots of noises in the house, but she was too
scared to go inside.
Lily hugged Coco tight!

A car pulled up outside the house.
A lady got out of the car and knocked on the door.
The lady went inside and Lily heard her mommy crying.
Coco licked Lily's cheek.

The lady told Lily she had to go stay
some where for a little while until it was safe.
Her mommy was crying and her Daddy was yelling mean things.
Lily did not want to leave Coco.
Lily was sad.

The lady took Lily away from her mommy and daddy,
so that she could be safe.

The lady told her she would be staying with
Ms. Shea. Ms. Shea did not have any kids or pets.

Ms. Shea's house had a big play room.
Lily found a bed with a pink blanket, which was her favorite color.
Lily saw a box full of toys and ran to play.

After it got dark, Lily wanted to go home.
She missed Coco. She had never been away from Coco.
Lily began to cry.
Ms. Shea tried to calm her down, but she was too sad.

The next few days Lily did not want to play
with any toys.
Lily did not like Ms. Shea.
Lily missed her mommy, daddy and Coco.
Ms. Shea bought Lily candy, a baby doll and even a trampoline.
Nothing made Lily happy because she missed her family.

Ms. Shea told Lily she would get to have visits with
her mommy and daddy.
Lily was happy, but she missed Coco.
Coco was not allowed to come with her mommy and daddy
but her mommy showed her pictures of Coco on her phone.

Lily missed Coco so much.
When it was time to leave, Lily got sad, but her mommy told her
she would see her again.

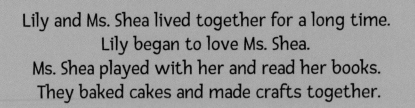

Lily and Ms. Shea lived together for a long time.
Lily began to love Ms. Shea.
Ms. Shea played with her and read her books.
They baked cakes and made crafts together.

There was no fighting or yelling in Ms. Shea's house.
Even though Lily missed her family, she
felt safe with Ms. Shea.

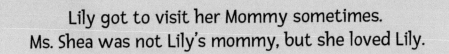

Lily got to visit her Mommy sometimes.
Ms. Shea was not Lily's mommy, but she loved Lily.

Lily learned that she could have lots of people love her.
Ms. Shea loved Lily like a daughter and Lily felt
like she had two mommies that loved her.

Foster Care Facts:

There are currently more than 400,000 children in foster care in the United States.

Neglect is the #1 reason children are removed from the home.

Children in foster care wait 3-4 years, or more, to be adopted.

On average, a child can spend almost 12 to 20 months in foster care.

The average age of a foster child entering foster care is 7 to 8 years old.

51% of children in foster care reunify with their parents or primary caregivers.

44% of foster children are White, 23% African American, and 21% Hispanic.

Foster youth are seven times more likely than non-foster youth to have depression, and five times more likely to have anxiety.

One out of every five people who age out of the foster care system lack a home when they turn 18.

By the time foster youth are 24, only half of them will have stable and steady employment. The same percentage develop substance abuse.

Get the facts: Foster Care & Adoption.
American SPCC. (2021, September 10).
Retrieved from
https://americanspcc.org/get-the-facts-foster-care/

Made in the USA
Middletown, DE
26 November 2022

16124058R00020